50 MYTHS FOR HMO LANDLORDS

A List of the Top 50 Misconceptions about the HMO Business

By C.J. Haliburton BA, DMS Cert Ed
Proprietor of 156 HMOs and over 1000 tenants

The Myth Buster
WARNING: Reading this book could seriously increase your wealth

HMO Daddy
14 Walsall Road
Wednesbury
West Midlands
WS10 9JL

Print Edition
British Library Cataloguing in Publication Data.

A catalogue record for this book is available from the British Library.
Cover design and formatting by Oxford Literary Consultancy

Contents

DISCLAIMER

Jim Haliburton, known as the HMO Daddy, is neither a lawyer nor a financial advisor nor does the following represent legal or financial advice. If such advice is needed then the reader should seek the appropriate professional guidance from qualified experts with appropriate public liability insurance. The following information is given to the best of Jim Haliburton's knowledge as correct and is provided for educational purposes only. It is the reader's responsibility to obtain their own professional advice.

ACKNOWLEDGEMENT

Welcome to the first edition of *50 Myths for HMO Landlords*. My aim with *50 Myths for HMO Landlords* is to inform other HMO landlords and those thinking of entering the HMO market of many of the misconceptions in the business.

The HMO business can be a lonely road, with seemingly no one to turn to or without anyone who is able to understand the problems HMO landlords encounter. We, as landlords, are often vilified by the press, not to mention the unreasonable persecution by Local Authority Housing Standards Departments, whose efforts could be more productively utilised improving their own appalling housing.

The journey to becoming an HMO landlord may be hard, but there is light at the end of the tunnel. With house price inflation, you should make a good return on selling up, though I do not think selling would be a sensible thing to do – after all, why leave a business which becomes increasingly profitable?

I would like to thank Toni Neal for typing up numerous manuscripts, Bingbing Chang, Sam Maddrell, Hannah Moodie, Manoj Tailor, Joshua Haliburton and Lise Pratt and others for their proof-reading and comments, but any mistakes are entirely down to me. Might I also thank my family and our dog for preserving my sanity.

C.J. Haliburton
November 2018

ABOUT JIM HALIBURTON

Jim began buying property in 1991, when he was a college lecturer. He started by letting a house to students and slowly built up a small portfolio of student lets. Business changed in 1995 and he lost most of his students because the college changed the way it provided accommodation. Instead, he focussed on working tenants and continued to grow a portfolio of HMOs, also known as shared houses or multi lets. He now manages over 156 HMOs. Having left his job as a lecturer in 2004, he continued his passion for lecturing and education by writing *A Guide to Becoming a Multi-Millionaire HMO Landlord* in 2005, which maintains its status as the leading manual on the subject of HMOs. He is in demand as a speaker on the property circuit, running courses and mentorships. Jim has also written multiple books on the subject of being an HMO landlord and the methods of acquiring property. He is also available for private consultations.

Jim has published the following manuals, guides and books:

MANUALS

A Guide to Becoming a Multi-Millionaire HMO Landlord

Operating Standards for HMO Landlords

*DIY Eviction – a Guide on How to Legally,
Quickly and Cheaply Evict Tenants*

Forms, Notices and Letters for HMO Landlords

A Guide to Letting to the Unemployed

BOOKS

35 Money-Making or Saving Tips for HMO Landlords

The Rules for HMO Landlords

Planning and HMOs

HMOs and Compensation for Unlawful Eviction

HMO Daddy Reveals All

An Introduction for HMO Landlords to Letting to the Unemployed

101 Questions and Answers for HMO Landlords

More Questions and Answers for HMO Landlords

Even More 101 Questions and Answers for HMO Landlords

A Compendium of HMO Daddy Blogs

INTRODUCTION

Welcome to the first edition of *50 Myths for HMO Landlords*. Though written primarily for HMO landlords, some of what I have written applies to the whole of the private rented sector. I write because I like it and it is a form of relaxation; I started to write this book over Christmas 2017. I hope you find it interesting and stimulating. In this business, we need to constantly challenge what we are doing to survive.

Over the years, I have noticed among the majority of landlords a great reluctance to try and understand their own business. There is little questioning of the status quo or wish to get involved in landlord affairs. The membership of landlord associations is in the single percentage figures. Upon questioning the average landlord, the most common refrain is, "what is in it for me?" or "what do I get?" The rules and laws governing the business are generally unquestioned. There is no attempt to understand the science of what is done or how the business can be improved. "I have always done it this way," is the general, unquestioning response. There seems to be a passive acceptance of regulations because the government says it is good.

The science behind being a landlord is archaic! If medicine were practised at the same level it would be called witchcraft. Two examples below illustrate my point:

The first is before the Tenancy Deposit Scheme was introduced, I stopped taking deposits – mostly because deposits made no difference to my tenants' behaviour. Yes, common sense says the deposits should stop tenants from damaging the property and encourage them to return the property in good condition. I analysed the thousands of tenants I had housed over prior decades and found no correlation between taking deposits and the state of the property at the end of the tenancy. It is now a decade since I stopped taking deposits and I still detect no difference in tenant behaviour. My findings beg the question: why do landlords still take deposits, especially given the administration involved and the severe penalties for failure to comply? Therefore, I do not see how deposits are beneficial. I have spoken on the topic for over ten years and the answer to my question "why do you take deposits?" is always the same: "because I always have," "surely it must work," and or "because everyone does it."

The second example is energy conservation. I pay for the heating in most of my HMOs (over 156 properties) and there is no reduction in the bills I pay between properties with so-called energy-saving methods such as double glazing, wall and roof insulation, and energy-efficient boilers. I am not claiming double glazing, wall and roof insulation do not have other benefits, but what concerns HMO landlords who pay the bills is: will they save money? Money saving is crucial. Why landlords do not save money should be a topic of investigation. I can see no redeeming benefits in using energy-efficient boilers except they improve the properties' EPC rating, but that just questions of the value of EPC ratings.

Enjoy.

MYTH ONE

You cannot get all your money and more out of a deal

That you cannot get all your money out of a deal is the big one where I am so often questioned. People assume that to buy property you have to leave money in the deal. I can and do get all my money out of a deal and often a lot more. I have written a lot on this myth. In the area where I operate, an HMO has a greater value as a business than it does as a house. Even taking into account the cost of converting the property, I still get back everything I spend using commercial lending: i.e. I leave no money in the property and better yet, still make a profit after paying the mortgage and all expenses.

I accept that creating a small HMO and getting it valued on income is now proving increasingly difficult. To be on the safe side, it is best to use ex-commercial buildings to improve the possibility of ensuring the property is valued on income. I should warn you that getting all of your money out of a deal has never been guaranteed; just because I have done it does not mean you can do it. By that, I do not mean you will not be able to do it; I am never sure even I can repeat my success even though I have done it over 200 times. Occasionally, it takes more than one attempt to successfully reclaim all of your money.

MYTH TWO
Energy conservation saves money

The myth in question is one where I am nearly always disbelieved. I have tried a number of energy-saving strategies such as the installation of loft and wall insulation, double glazing, energy-efficient boilers – none make any difference to the gas bill (nearly all my properties are heated by gas). The amount of gas used to heat the property remains the same as it had before the installation of loft and wall insulation, double glazing, or an energy-efficient boiler. I provide 24/7 central heating in most of my HMOs, and so I expected to see significant savings from these measures, yet I found no change. I might also add that light timers, LED bulbs, and energy-efficient electric heaters, make little or no difference in electricity consumption.

I am not claiming that insulation does not have positive side effects such as reducing condensation and mould, or that it increases the comfort of a property or reduces noise, but the point I am making is that it does not save landlord's money.

MYTH THREE
Housing standards are of benefit

Apart from fire-resistant foam in furniture, I can find no evidence that what Housing Standards impose on me as an HMO landlord do anything to save lives or injury or improves the health of my tenants. I look upon Housing Standards as a tax on being an HMO landlord.

Room sizes are one typical example – the minimum legal size for a room is 65 sq. ft./6.51 sq. m. This is being enforced enthusiastically despite there being no evidence that a smaller room is harmful to a person or that a larger room is beneficial. Indeed, the larger room will cost more to heat. I am not comparing tenants to prisoners, but we imprison criminals in prison cells of 32 sq. ft. and this is considered to be humane. People are sent to prison as a punishment, not to be punished, and they are forced to spend up to 23 hours in their cells. Yet on the outside, where tenants are free to choose what size accommodation they wish to live in and pay for, it must be at least twice the size of a prison cell.

MYTH FOUR

Gas safety saves lives

I question the claim that gas safety regulations imposed on landlords save six lives a year in rented accommodation, as there is no great number of deaths due to gas in the owner-occupied sector where many of the regulations imposed on landlords do not apply.

Conversely, up to 30,000 people die each year due to the cold. The over-regulation of gas has turned a lot of landlords off the idea of fitting gas. I estimate that the cost of using gas central heating in an HMO is about a fifth of the cost of using electric heating. The extortionate cost of electrical heating leaves people with the stark choice of freezing or starving to death – it appears they choose to freeze. This is the unintended consequence of gas safety regulations, including an annual gas safety check.

Also flawed is the targeting of all gas appliances. Balanced flue appliances rarely present a problem – it is generally only the old-style gas fires that use chimneys and take air from the room that kill. The issues of death from carbon monoxide poisoning could have been solved easily by banning non-balanced flue heaters in rented properties.

MYTH FIVE
Having central heating attracts tenants

As long as the property is reasonably dry and warm, I find it makes no difference to the rent charged, the lettability, or the retention of tenants whether you supply inclusive central heating or not. I agree this defies logic, but I have tested my hypothesis and it works. Be warned: the house must be naturally dry and warm for this to work; otherwise you will have issues with mould, and yes, tenants will leave if the house is cold and damp. I emphasise that the tenants must be told that there is no central heating in the property before they move in or enter into a tenancy. You will cause a lot of problems if you try and remove the heating afterwards and the house must be normally dry.

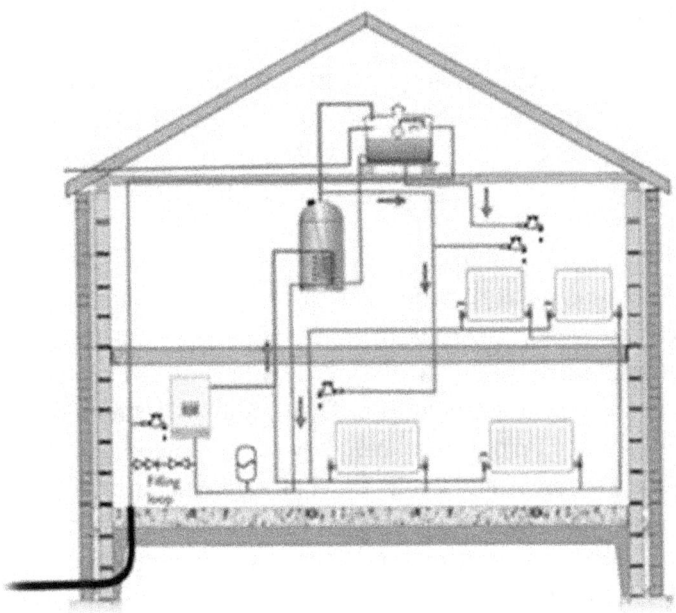

MYTH SIX

Tenants object to paying Council Tax

Put aside for one moment the insane merits of councils charging Council Tax on each room in an HMO – i.e. treating each as a separate house or flat when charging Council Tax. From the council's point of view, charging Council Tax on each room is a highly attractive proposition since it imposes a substantial increase in tax revenue. Even if all the tenants claim single person relief of 25%, the Council Tax from a six-bed HMO increases substantially. Assuming the house was a band A and the Council Tax on the house is £1k pa (the largest band chargeable, however small the property), if each of the six rooms will be banded for Council Tax band A at £1k pa (6 x £1k x 75% single occupancy relief) = £4,500, the council receives an extra £3,500 in tax providing the tenants pay.

Bizarrely, I find that it makes no difference to the rent charged, the lettability of the room, or the retention rate of tenants compared to properties where the Council Tax is inclusive if tenants are told **before** they move in that they have to pay their own Council Tax.

Other landlords say that if tenants have to pay their own Council Tax then it must make a difference to the rent that can be charged, but invariably they have not tried letting where their tenants pay their own Council Tax. However, I have and do let rooms where the tenant pays the Council Tax. The landlords I speak to do not believe it makes zero difference. They say it is illogical and that if they were a tenant, they would expect a rent reduction if they paid their own Council Tax. I agree with them – so would I – but we are landlords, not tenants. It only makes a difference if the tenant has to start paying the Council Tax **after** they have moved in and the change takes place while they are in occupation. They start the tenancy being told the landlord pays and during their tenancy they find they then have to pay; this makes an enormous difference. In such a situation, I find it best to pay the Council Tax myself. I find it only does not make any difference if the tenant is told they have to pay Council Tax **before** they move in.

Further, I would not advocate having rooms banded for Council Tax even though the landlord will save having to pay Council Tax on the whole house (if all the rooms are banded for Council Tax, the landlord does not have to pay the Council Tax on the HMO). They will be landed with a lot of extra administration and now have to pay the Council Tax on void rooms.

MYTH SEVEN
Varying the rent charged affects demand

Knowing how much rent to charge is difficult. I find that reducing the rent charged makes little difference to demand. If there is demand, the property will let and there is a ceiling to rent levels. Breach the ceiling and though wanted, the property will be difficult to let.

Essentially dropping your rents serves only to reduce your profit, not your voids. Ten percent voids are better than dropping your rents by 10% as you will still not fill all of your rooms and more tenants mean more costs. If a whole property is empty, you may wish to charge less, but do not charge less universally. Beware of charging lower rates to entice new tenants into a partially-full house as it will cause problems with existing tenants if you charge a new tenant in the same house less than the existing tenants are paying – unless there is justification for the reduction (such as it being a smaller or less popular room). Property is not like holidays, trains, and flights. Tenants will not accept discriminatory pricing.

MYTH EIGHT

Keep the property nice and the tenants will look after it

I can find no evidence of this from the 1,000-plus rooms I let. Just because a property is in beautiful condition does not mean that it gets looked after any better than an old, tired property. The benefit of a well-dressed property in good condition is it lets a lot better.

Whether or not a property is looked after comes down to the tenant – some will care for your property, others will not.

MYTH NINE

Provide a high standard of property and tenants will stay longer

I can find no evidence from the analysis of the 1,000-plus rooms I provide to support this, in fact the contrary. I have properties that are in very poor condition – mainly because tenants have been in the property for so long and it has not been renovated. If I try and renovate the property, this often upsets my tenants and I have had long-term tenants leave.

Conversely, we get more turnover in my five-star properties. Tenants churn is more to do with their employment. For example, contractors leave when their job finishes, however nice the property is. The tenants who will stay long-term are often unemployed and usually do not do much to care for their rooms.

MYTH TEN

Valuers can value

One of the great myths in this business is that surveyors will give consistent valuations. Ask ten surveyors to value a property and you will receive eleven widely-ranging answers. Within a period of two months, I had the same property valued at zero, £70k, £140k and £200k. I once bought a property for £80k and one surveyor valued it at what I paid for it. Six weeks later, another surveyor valued the same property for £200k, but nothing had changed! In hiring a surveyor, you essentially pay for a personal opinion.

Banks will sue surveyors if they get a valuation wrong, so a surveyor will, in order to defend themselves, have to show they carried out due diligence by checking comparable properties. Comparables are what other HMOs in the area recently sold for and are used to justify their valuation. Lenders may also guide the surveyor to whatever value they deem appropriate. Some surveyors just want to get paid and not risk their liability insurance, which I believe gives them an incentive to down-value.

MYTH ELEVEN

Treat your tenants well and they will look after the property and pay the rent on time

My observation of tenants does not support this, but I have never knowingly tried to treat my tenants badly. Landlords should treat their tenants well because it is the right thing to do. Whether a tenant looks after a property has more to do with the type of tenant. As for rent arrears, I have come across some very nasty landlords who have told me that they have no rent arrears and I have believed them. I will not sink to their level and I suggest you do not either, if you wish to stay in this game for any length of time (i.e. long enough to make some serious money with the capital appreciation that property provides). Having your property looked after and your rent paid on time has all to do with selecting the right tenant and firm but fair management. If a tenant refuses to pay rent, then evict them immediately. They will not suddenly start to pay if you leave it for a few months.

MYTH TWELVE

Repair the property and the tenants will stay

I follow up my tenants when they leave and find little evidence to say their leaving was prompted by our failure to repair or renovate properties. I am not saying this is never the case, but it is very rarely the case. Some of my tenants have commended me for carrying out repairs promptly and they tell me how much better I am than their previous landlord. However, they never say they moved to me because of poor maintenance by their previous landlord. They always move because of their job or some external factor, not because the landlord was slow or refused to carry out repairs.

Do not misunderstand me: it is the landlord's legal and moral obligation to carry out repairs. It is also crucial to protect oneself against potential disrepair claims to record all requests for repairs from your tenants and promptly attend to them, but failure to repair does not cause significant loss of tenants. It probably only has a marginal impact on a tenant who was going to leave anyway and hastens them leaving.

MYTH THIRTEEN

You get what you pay for

I can find no link between the price of fittings, furniture, materials, utilities, insurance, and services and the quality or longevity of a product or service. HMO Daddy's Top Tip: save your money by shopping around and checking out the quality and value as best as you can. Do not let price be guide of quality.

MYTH FOURTEEN

Councils encourage the supply and are protective of housing

BEWARE

DYSFUNCTIONAL
UNCARING COUNCILS

You might assume that councils would be supportive of a project to develop a derelict building into useful low-cost housing for which there is enormous demand, but this is not the case. You only have to be in the HMO business for a few minutes to realise that councils rarely support the supply of housing. The main objectors are usually the planners. At best, council officials are indifferent, but outright opposition happens, especially if the property is being turned into an HMO. Councils can be very dysfunctional. Departments do not work together, bureaucracy rules and petty in-fighting and empire-building are rife. I find it amazing that the truth of this is not better known. To give two examples:

The first example is: the government and councils make much of rogue landlords, yet the biggest offenders of Housing Standards are the councils themselves. There are far more complaints about the state of council housing than private housing. The people who keep the statistics are the council themselves, who classify complaints about their own housing as "requests for service" yet count any contact from a tenant of a private landlord as a complaint. Worse than this, the councils police the private sector and ignore their own massive failings. No one questions the council unless you get a failing on the size of the Grenfell Tower disaster.

The second example is homelessness. One of the significant causes of tenants losing their homes is the bureaucracy of the housing benefit system, now called universal credit, which appears to operate where it can to ensure that landlords do not get paid. The result is that tenants are unable to access housing or are evicted as their housing benefit is not paid. It is unfortunate that councils can be poor in paying housing benefit or try to unjustifiably reclaim rent payments paid to the landlord when instead they should be supporting landlords to keep the tenants housed.

MYTH FIFTEEN

Lenders are consistent

Lenders vary their approach to lending all the time, especially in regard to HMOs, and do not always announce their policy changes in advance. It is often only when you apply and get turned down for the loan, or the loan is not what you were expecting, that you realise that a particular lender no longer wishes to lend (or at least not lend on the same terms as they had previously). So much is at the discretion of the bank's underwriter.

BE CONSISTENT

MYTH SIXTEEN

It is hard to evict a tenant

We constantly hear it is difficult to evict a tenant. However, after I had employed a solicitor to do a few evictions, I realised that most of the problems, as so many things in this business, were caused by solicitors. The main issues were: the time they took to do anything, the cost, and their obsession with detail. To quote one solicitor I dealt with, they "would only present a properly and thoroughly prepared case."

I looked at the eviction process and I set up my own system that allows me to get a possession order in nine weeks, and I have since carried out over 350 evictions with 100% success. When I used solicitors, it often took me weeks just to book a meeting with the solicitor and request them to issue proceedings. I quickly realised that it is easy to evict a tenant, provided that you follow the correct procedure. One of the leading landlords' associations says that it takes on average nine months to evict a tenant and costs £2,500, but this does not have to be the case. A tenant can be evicted easily, quickly, and cheaply using my DIY eviction process (see www.hmodaddy.com for my DIY eviction manual that explains my system and it is the only DIY eviction manual on the market). It normally only takes me nine weeks to get a possession order.

In my view, nine weeks is too long to wait to get a possession order; it should only take days to evict a tenant. The reason I say this is that the harm one bad tenant can cause in an HMO is incredible – I have had a whole property cleared by one bad tenant. When evicting a tenant, there is a very bureaucratic process that must be followed correctly if you are to succeed, not including the time it can take to get a bailiff to remove a tenant if they refuse to leave. The delay in getting county court bailiffs to act is also a major cause of concern.

I find it surprising I have to evict so many tenants as I have a "no eviction" policy and will not evict a tenant just because they are unable to pay the rent. I only seek their removal if they wilfully refuse to pay or refuse to co-operate with us in helping to get them paid by claiming housing benefit. Usually, the defaulting tenants are also causing us problems as well such as anti-social behaviour. That I have to evict tenants only goes to show the attitude of a small minority of my tenants who do not value their tenancies.

EVICTION NOTICE
(NOTICE TO QUIT)

Date:		Tenant:			
Address:		City		State/Zip	

YOU HAVE VIOLATED YOUR LEASE WHEN YOU

☐ Non payment of rent
☐ Damaged the property
☐ Moved in new tenants and/or tenants living there that are not on the lease
☐ Abandoned the above-referenced address

In Section _____ of your lease it states tenant is not to deliberately, or negligently destroy, deface, damage, or remove any part of the property or grounds. In damaging the property, the tenant has breached the lease.

In Section _____ of your lease it states the maximum number of people that can occupy the property is ___. Only those people listed in this lease can occupy the stated property. No new tenants can move in without the Landlord's written approval. In moving new tenants without the Landlord's permission, you have violated your Lease Agreement.

If you do not leave the leased premises and give possession of the leased premises to the landlord within 15 days, landlord will begin a lawsuit in court to have you removed from the leased premises.

_____
Landlord Signature

POSTED BY:

☐ delivering a copy of notice to the named tenant.

☐ posting a copy of the notice on the main door of the property, no one actually being present at the residence.

LAFM009

MYTH SEVENTEEN

It is easy to make money in property

Although there have been cases of people making money very easily and quickly, for most it generally takes over a decade to make significant wealth from property. The headline income from HMOs initially looks good, but after maintenance, voids, and bad debts, the residual profit can be slight, especially if the property is not self-managed.

Capital appreciation is often the real benefit with property and this normally takes years to accrue. Although it is not grindingly hard work operating an HMO, there are many stresses and setbacks on the way. To succeed in the property business, one must be able to act incredibly quickly when the right deal arises and accept often unquantifiable risks. A good deal is often nothing more than gut instinct.

MYTH EIGHTEEN

You need money to get into property

That money helps is undeniable. However, not having money is not a disabling barrier. It just requires a lot more work, knowledge, and luck to find the right deal, and you need to think things through thoroughly and creatively. Most investors turn to using "no money deals" only when they have run out of money, but there is nothing to prevent investors using them to start with. The biggest obstacle to starting without money is people themselves who don't believe that no or little money down strategies exist or that they can get deals. They refuse to believe that someone will hand over a property for little or no money.

On the bright side, having too much money can be a curse as it allows you to thoughtlessly blunder into buying a "money pit" (a property that incurs on-going costs for years) or a "vanity buy" (a property that looks good but generates little or no income).

MYTH NINETEEN
It is hard to find good deals

I say that good deals are hidden in plain sight, but people refuse to accept such a fact. They insist in believing that there is some special secret formula to finding good deals, when, in fact, you cannot hide a building – buildings are just there! It is mainly that people lack imagination or the belief that they can be made to work. Often, a good deal is obvious when viewed in hindsight. For instance, when a derelict building is transformed into a profit-making property, how come the same building sat empty, sometimes for decades?

MYTH TWENTY

People will not give you their properties for nothing

It is true people will not normally give you a property for nothing. You need to offer them something they want more than money. Such an offer must address the owner's problems – using strategies such as delayed completion, lease options, leases, or vendor finance. In other words, you normally pay later but pay nothing up front. With commercial properties, the biggest motivating factor I find is the business rates. The owner will happily hand over the keys and being paid is secondary, providing you accept responsibility for the business rates. The possible exception is adverse possession, but that is normally based on the owner being untraceable or no longer existing.

For more on how to get properties for nothing, get my book 'How to get properties for free and cash-flow for thousands' only available from www.hmodaddy.com.

MYTH TWENTY-ONE

It is easy to get joint venture partners to fund deals

A joint venture is a situation where (usually) one partner puts in the money and the other does the work and manages the property, though it can be whatever the parties agree.

I have, at last count, 32 joint venture partners and love them all, but getting them takes enormous time and patience. Of five people showing significant interest, only one agrees to do a deal with me. Fifty percent of those who agree to proceed – even paying a deposit – withdraw; an additional twenty percent will pull out during the deal. In short, it can be a very frustrating and time-consuming process. Compare JV partners with approaching a bank: I find I can usually agree a deal in principle within minutes and banks rarely renege on a deal with me, once agreed (but they can be very pedantic).

I am not suggesting to avoid collaboration in joint ventures – it may be the only option – but joint venturing requires an enormous amount of time and effort, as with most things in property.

MYTH TWENTY-TWO
You need planning permission

Another old chestnut. Contrary to popular perception, there is no enforceable law that says you have to apply for planning permission. It is there to ensure that the council will not object to a particular development or use. However, one would be very reckless to build a property not knowing whether the planning department will object and could take enforcement action and make you take the building down. Beware: building a property just six inches too high has been used as justification for refusing planning permission or taking enforcement action.

Doing something without planning permission is not a crime. The criminal offence only arises where enforcement action is brought and not complied with. Bringing enforcement action is the only thing the planners can do if they find you have not applied for planning permission, which they are not supposed to do unless the development is causing serious harm to the amenity. Serious harm to the amenity is very subjective and could be what a planner regards as an eyesore or has the potential to create problems without any proof that they will! I would advise against going to any great expense without first obtaining planning permission. For more on planning permission see my book *HMOs and Planning* available from www.hmodaddy.com.

MYTH TWENTY-THREE

Tenants will pay the rent asked

The rent you can charge for the same room can vary widely. In one notable example, I had a property with eight rooms but had little idea of what rent to charge, so I charged what I needed to cover my costs. I advertised the rent being, 'from £40 per week.' I quickly realised that there was good demand for the rooms, so I increased the rent at each let. By the time I had filled the building, the least popular room let for £80 per week.

Our rent on certain rooms can fluctuate by between £90 per week and £120 per week – an incredible 33% difference. The rent charged on a particular property often comes down to nothing more than intuition or gut feeling.

MYTH TWENTY-FOUR

Councils can be trusted

The biggest competitor to the private rented sector is councils, whether they directly provide the housing or via a housing trust. Amazingly, the councils also police and control the supply of housing through the planning system and Housing Standards. This blatant conflict of interest would never be tolerated in another market. This is just one of the obstacles you will be choosing to face if you become a landlord, but at least you are forewarned.

MYTH TWENTY-FIVE

Councils know what they're doing

The level of incompetence in council Housing Standards Departments is unbelievable. Most of the time Housing Standards officers survive because people believe they are right and comply, but if you challenge them, you will be amazed just how often they have it wrong. When the Housing Act 2004 introduced the Residential Property Tribunal (RPT), an appeal court against council's decisions – now replaced by the First Tier Tribunal (Property Division) – in nearly every case that was appealed by a landlord, the landlord won, and the council lost. Does it sound to you like the council knows what it is doing?

MYTH TWENTY-SIX

Single parents make the best tenants

A lot of landlords say the best tenants to have are single parents as they make good long-term tenants and turn the house into their home. My experience has been the exact opposite. I find that single parents look upon the private sector as temporary accommodation and that they (or their children) trash the house.

Generally, I find that single parents prefer to be housed by the council and will therefore find faults with my property or else not pay the rent, pleading unaffordability. They hope to be evicted, knowing that the council are under a duty to rehouse them. Councils who want to expand their empire have an incentive to encourage this behaviour so they can fill their own housing or create a waiting list and puts pressure on the government to increase the already vast funds they are given.

MYTH TWENTY-SEVEN

Single lets have fewer problems and tenants stay longer

How long a tenant stays depends upon the type of tenants you house in the first place. We house a lot of contractors who leave when their project finishes. If I remove contractors from my figures, I have proportionally more long-term HMO tenants than I have tenants in single-let houses and flats, but this is beginning to change, and I am finding greater stability with my single-let tenants.

I have analysed the churn from the 1,000-plus HMO tenants I house and the 22 single lets I have, hoping to identify types of tenants who pay, stay, and behave. So far, I have not identified a conclusive pattern, but I will continue researching as I want to produce an algorithm for identifying long-stay HMO tenants.

MYTH TWENTY-EIGHT
Demand for HMOs is easy to determine

Where there is enormous demand, it is usually easy to identify by putting a trial advertisement on Spareroom. However, I have discovered by accident that there is no way of conclusively checking that there is **no demand** for an HMO that I can identify, apart from setting up and advertising the HMO. For most people, buying a property and converting it into an HMO, hoping there will be demand for it, sounds like a recipe for disaster. However, having developed properties into HMOs so many times, I have become slightly blasé about it. Creating HMOs for which demand is unknown rarely causes me any concern, apart from when I am asked whether it will let. I can only reply, "I hope so."

I would not take the risk of investing a lot of money in a property if I had no knowledge of its likely demand. I will only take a chance on letting cheap or free properties that I can easily convert into an HMO. For example, I would not hesitate to accept a house in reasonable condition on a lease option, with a short break clause in my favour, provided that I only had to pay a nominal deposit and initially no or very little rent. I would take such a property on and just hope that I would be able to let it. Bear in mind, I have a substantial portfolio producing a surplus and my scale, experience, and network insulates me from the risk of such speculative investments. Buying without confidence that it will let is not an approach I would recommend to a new investor without any of my advantages.

MYTH TWENTY-NINE

You can identify a potentially bad tenant

I always say to those who think they are a good judge of people that they should come and work in my letting office for a month and see how many times they misjudge those who apply for accommodation. The worst case I came across in my early days was a pleasant, polite, presentable man who turned out to be a drug addict with a speciality of robbing old-age pensioners. He had just been released from prison and soon afterwards returned. My new lettings manager had assured me that he was a good judge of character and yet let to this nightmare tenant. We have now introduced processes to prevent this type of thing from happening again.

When you are dealing with people, you can never be 100% correct as there are just too many variables. The more questions you ask and the more checking you do, the less likely you are to judge incorrectly, but this does not get round the problem where people change. Though it is unusual that people change, it does happen. Oddly, losing his or her job causes problems, though it shouldn't cause more than a hiccup in the rent as the tenant can claim housing benefit (now called Universal Credit) and this covers their rent. The main cause of problems is that the tenant refuses to claim housing benefit, or they claim it and then keep it without ever paying the landlord. Other causes of problems include a breakdown of a relationship and mental illness. I find these events are intertwined: the loss of employment can often be caused by unsatisfactory work or illness, and if it is not, a job loss can lead to a relationship breaking up and illness.

MYTH THIRTY

You can enter the tenant's room by giving 24 hours' notice

Giving 24 hours' notice (or notice of any length) does **not** entitle the landlord to enter the tenant's room without permission. The tenant can still refuse access. When a property is let, it effectively becomes the tenant's property subject to the conditions imposed by the landlord in the tenancy agreement (the main condition being the payment of rent). If the tenant breaks any of the conditions, all the landlord can do is evict the tenant, which takes months. Theoretically, a tenant's refusal to allow landlord access to their room would be grounds to evict, though I doubt that many judges would grant a possession order on such a ground – I myself have never tried it. I just accept the tenant's wishes.

MYTH THIRTY-ONE

A landlord has control over their tenants

It is the view of those who have influence over the government that landlords have control over their tenants, which is nonsense. Once a tenant occupies a property, a landlord has no more control over them than a car rental company has over the way the person hiring the car drives. The idea of making landlords responsible for the behaviour of their tenants is as daft as making car hire companies responsible for the behaviour of drivers who borrow their cars or a supermarket for the way its canned stock is cooked or used by the shopper.

In reality, all a landlord could do with a tenant exhibiting anti-social behaviour within their tenancy would be an eviction. Their power in such a predicament is severely restricted by legislation and comes with a lengthy and costly procedure. Even an anti-social tenant's protection against eviction is sacrosanct and only goes to show the distorted thinking the legislators have about landlords. The notion that landlords are able to control their tenants and should be responsible for their actions is a gross distortion of the landlord's powers and part of the chattering hysteria perpetrated by local authorities, who are our main competitors and seek to discredit private landlords. Worse, when anti-social behaviour is examined, it is found mostly to be caused by social landlord tenants, the biggest provider being councils.

MYTH THIRTY-TWO
The homeless cannot find accommodation

Firstly, allow me to note that there is a distinction between rough sleepers and those currently without permanent accommodation, such as those in council-provided hostels awaiting housing, all of whom are classed as homeless. The following relates to the former, although I stress that I do not wish to disparage those who are genuinely homeless or have difficulty in finding somewhere to live. That said, I wonder whether those living publicly on the streets are homeless or if homelessness is a choice? If I were to be homeless – and I have been – the last place I would choose to sleep would be publicly on the streets. At any one time I have about one hundred void units, which is embarrassing and loses me money. However, I know the social sector has a lot more voids (yet another of their guilty secrets).

I would, and I have, let my empty rooms to anyone without charging a deposit or any money upfront and helped the tenant to claim housing benefit or its replacement, Universal Credit. We have and will supply food, toiletries, clothing, and kitchen utensils to those in need. The only criteria we impose is that we must be confident the person will treat the property in a tenant-like manner, which means behaving and co-operating in claiming Housing Benefit. Unfortunately, nearly every rough sleeper I have housed has failed to co-operate in claiming Housing Benefit and has wrecked the room and usually abandons it for the streets – this, all in spite of providing support for such tenants. Perhaps my support or accommodation was not suitable, but what cannot be contested is that my working tenants choose my accommodation (and pay for it) and they have a choice as to where they live.

Please do not take the above as any criticism of those who work and help the homeless. Homelessness it is a terrible thing and just because many abuse the situation does not mean we should not try and help those who we can; you never know of the challenges some homeless people may face.

My doors are still open to any homeless person who needs accommodation. That many abuse the situation does not mean we should stop trying to help those who want help. I will continue to offer accommodation to homeless people, provided that I am satisfied that they will treat the property, the other tenants, and my staff with respect, and pay or cooperate in claiming housing benefit (which will pay their rent on their behalf). However, very rarely is my offer accepted. I do not think many people appreciate that people living on the streets has little to do with the lack of housing (and I am not saying there is not a lack of housing).

MYTH THIRTY-THREE

Money motivates staff

A widely-held belief is that staff can be inspired to work harder or to work more productively by incentives like increased pay. The truth is that monetary incentives only occasionally work in the long-term. In reality, staff have an expectation of what they should earn. Paying commission simply means they reach their target amount earlier, at which point they stop putting the effort into working. People may say they work for the money, but the reality is much more complicated. Generally, if they could earn what they want by, say, Tuesday, they will coast from Wednesday to Friday. Motivating staff is a lot more complex than simply increasing pay. I recommend researching Maslow's Hierarchy of Needs if you are interested in the theory of the complexity of motivating staff.

I will provide a classic example by using a taxi analogy: have you ever wondered why it is difficult to order a taxi when it is raining? Most people assume it is because there is more demand for taxis on a rainy day, which is true, but the increased demand is compounded by there being fewer taxis on the roads on a rainy day. Research shows this is because many taxi drivers have an amount they wish to earn on a daily basis and that they go home once they earn that amount. When it is raining, there is a greater demand for taxis, so the drivers hit their daily targets earlier and then go home, leading to fewer available taxis.

MYTH THIRTY-FOUR

Loyalty to a product or service is repaid

Despite the opportunity for substantial savings, loyalty or inertia prevents most people from changing service or product provider. I gladly share with other landlords my insurance and utility providers (whom I have chosen because they are the cheapest), but only those who do not have the service already take advantage of my offer.

I have found no evidence to show that if you are a long-term user of a product or service you would get any better service than a new customer, so it pays to shop around on renewal.

MYTH THIRTY-FIVE

Deposits are worth taking

I have found only marginal evidence that tenants will take greater care of my property just because they paid a deposit. Even without a deposit, if damage is caused to the property then the landlord can always sue the ex-tenant. I think deposits are charged solely by convention. Admittedly, you could use the deposit as a free loan (though technically this is wrong, and the deposit should be kept in a ring-fenced account). For me, the hassle of having to deal with the tenancy deposit regulations, the penalties for failure to comply, the evidence needed should you wish to withhold the deposit, and the risk of the deposit going to adjudication makes the taking of deposits uneconomical.

Instead, I now charge an administration fee and keep it, though it looks like the charging of administration fees is going to be outlawed in April 2019.

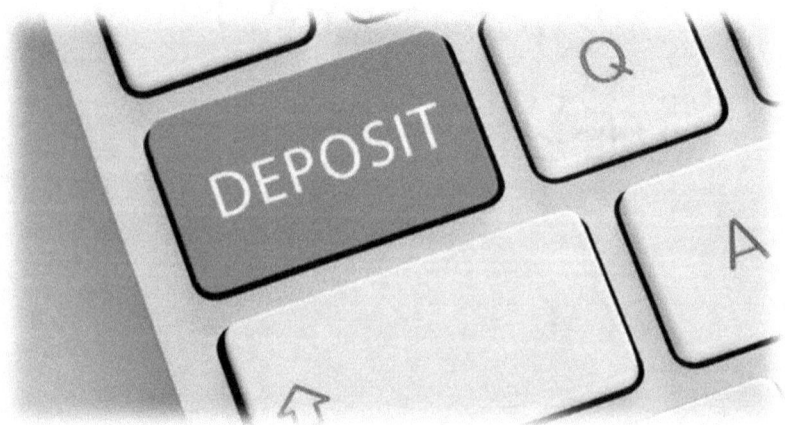

MYTH THIRTY-SIX

Inventories are worthwhile

Business should be about maximising income and minimising work. Inventories fail on both of these fronts. They do not bring in any extra income (though they may help to reduce loss), and they create lots of extra work (or at least the expense of an inventory clerk. If you add up the time and cost in making an inventory against the loss they prevent, they are not cost-effective in the market in which I operate. If you are letting a property with expensive fittings and furniture with a tenant you can sue, then there may be justification for having an inventory. In other words, whether it is worth taking an inventory or not depends on what you let and who you let to.

MYTH THIRTY-SEVEN
Thorough checking of tenants is cost effective

There are only four things about a tenant you need to check to avoid 99.8% of bad tenants. These are:

i. That they have the money to pay (and do pay) the rent and deposit (if charged) before they move in
ii. They are in full-time permanent work
iii. The rent is less than 50 percent of their take-home pay (i.e. affordable)
iv. They have no county court judgments

I do not check the last one (county court judgments). I used to, but I found most of my tenants did not have a credit history, so a credit check will turn up nothing shown. Further, checking beyond the four points will not significantly reduce the risk of default. Such checking is only of value when the above four criteria are not met.

The statistical evidence for the above criteria is from rent guarantee insurers who seem to assume that the tenants pay before they move in, but they don't check this. I find that the lack of a full-time job and the inability to pay fees in full before occupation are the main predictors of a defaulting tenant. Most of my tenants who default have not paid in full upfront, but this does not mean all tenants who are not able to pay upfront will default in paying their rent.

Now here comes the contradiction: when dealing with my properties, I do all I can to assess the tenants! I do not want to be in the 0.2% and so I include extra checks (despite what I said above). For more on assessing tenants effectively, see my *Operating Standards* – only available from www.hmodaddy.com.

MYTH THIRTY-EIGHT

Insurance is cost effective

The myth in question is probably one of the most controversial of all the matters I have mentioned. A landlord is better off self-insuring and saving the time of filling in claims forms and the cost of premiums – just suffer any losses as they come. The risk is not that great as shown by the statistics: building and contents insurers pay out less than one-fifth of the premiums collected in claims, so save yourself the insurer's profits and overheads.

The question you need to ask is that of Clint Eastwood in *Dirty Harry*: "Do you feel lucky?" Insurance has more to do with your attitude to risk, and I accept that a catastrophic risk could wipe you out, but so could other risks that are not insurable.

If you are borrowing money on property, it is a term of the loan that you have building insurance cover on the property, so I would shop around for the cheapest deal with the bare minimum of cover. Further, I advise that you do not claim for anything, or else you may pay back more in increased premiums over the coming years than you have claimed, if the insurer increases their premiums due to your claiming.

MYTH THIRTY-NINE
HMOs are easy to define

Not even Housing Standards officers are comfortable with defining what is and what is not an HMO. Most think you must have five occupiers, but this is incorrect: it is three or more inhabitants who occupy the property as their permanent place of accommodation; it is not the building that defines it as a HMO. There are many problems with such a definition, for example: what is permanent? Permanency often comes down to intention and can be very difficult to prove or disprove. It is generally accepted that if the occupier has a permanent home, or says they have a permanent home elsewhere, this is conclusive evidence that the tenant is not in permanent occupation. However, who says you cannot have two or more permanent places of occupation? Councils may request an occupier to sign a statement to say the place in which they are living is their permanent place of occupation. Such evidence is taken as conclusive when, in my view it is far from conclusive, as the tenant is usually following the instructions of the housing official. If you ask any of my HMO tenants whether they are intending to stay in my property permanently, they will all answer "no." I assume it is the same for other HMO landlords since very few HMO occupiers look upon their accommodation as permanent.

Then, what is meant by the term "occupiers" – is this person an occupier or just a guest of one of the other tenants, or are they a paying guest?

The status of lodgers is confused: it is questionable as to how many lodgers one needs for a property for it to become an HMO. (To be on the safe side, I would not have more than two lodgers in my house). However, many councils consider owner-occupied properties with lodgers as not being an HMO, which is incorrect. A property will be an HMO even with a live-in landlord.

The lay person tends to look at enforcement as the measure of what can or cannot be done, but how assiduously rules are applied is very variable. Most councils ignore HMOs with less than five tenants and lodgers, which is perhaps why I often meet people who wrongly tell me an HMO is five or more tenants, which is incorrect, as it is three or more unrelated tenants who are using the accommodation as their permanent accommodation that defines an HMO.

MYTH FORTY

When an HMO is licensable is clear cut

Ignore for the moment additional licensing (where all HMOs can be licensable) and selective licensing (where all rented property is licensable), both of which are at the discretion of the council to implement. Let us instead consider mandatory licensing, which is so-called because councils are required to implement it. Most landlords will say mandatory licencing applies when there are five or more tenants, or sometimes five or more bedrooms. However, the definition of a property that is subject to mandatory licencing states either the kitchen or bathroom, or both, must be shared and the occupiers treat the property as their permanent residence.

The general misconception is that a property becomes a licensable HMO when there are five or more occupiers. This is incorrect as there are three requirements that must be met for a property to be licensable. They are: i) 5 or more tenants, ii) the sharing of a kitchen or bathroom, and, iii) the tenants treat the property as their permanent residence.

NB: (1) As from 1st October 2018 the three-storey requirement was removed from the definition; previously, the property had to have three storeys.

(2) Students are an exception, though they are rarely permanent. The Housing Act states that they are permanent residents even though they may still consider their parents' home as their permanent residence.

MYTH FORTY-ONE

Housing Benefit is intended to pay the tenant's rent

We have a wonderful system in this country called Housing Benefit, where, if someone is unable to afford their rent, the Council will pay it. However, the system is gradually moving over to the government paying under another system called Universal Credit. Like so many wonderful ideas, it has unfortunately become overly bureaucratic, and the tail has for some time been wagging the dog – the purpose of ensuring the tenant had their rent paid has been lost.

In my experience, some people in council Housing Benefit Departments see their purpose to be as uncooperative and obstructive as they can to landlords and claimants. I refer to the Housing Benefit Department as the Department for Landlord Non-Payment. It is obvious from the remarks and behaviour of a few who work in housing benefit that they are very anti-landlord. It takes enormous persistence and administrative skills for landlords to ensure that they are paid, especially because it is the tenant's benefit. It is up to the tenant to make the claim for benefit, which some show little interest in doing.

To add to the difficulty of dealing with the administration of Housing Benefit, the government are wedded to the concept of creating financial responsibility in benefit tenants and insist the tenant should receive their rent directly before the tenant pays their landlord. Anyone with the slightest understanding of HMO benefit tenants will recognise this as complete nonsense. Most HMO tenants will **not** use the money they receive to pay their rent and end up being in rent arrears and eventually being evicted.

Worse, serial defaulters are not treated as criminals – despite a pattern of renting properties and not paying rent, despite having received housing benefit payment, which raises the presumption that they never intended to use the benefits to pay their landlord. No action is taken to stop tenants going from landlord to landlord claiming benefit and not paying their rent.

Conversely, the opposite applies with landlords and overpayments, along with suspected overpayments to landlords. These are pursued vigorously and automatically deducted from the rent paid to the landlord.

Further, tenants are encouraged **not** to pay their rent by some council officials and various tenancy support and legal organisations (often sponsored by the council), who tell the tenants that they have to be evicted by a long court process and do not have to pay the rent while being evicted. Also, tenants are often led to believe that they will be re-housed by the council once the bailiffs remove them from the property. Contrary to popular belief, it is – in my experience – relatively easy to have the rent paid to myself, the landlord, by Housing Benefit/Universal Credit for defaulting tenants. However, the landlord needs to apply, and in order to apply, the landlord needs to know the system and be persistent. The system is not user-friendly. It is strange that a government who says it wants to support landlords allows such a perverse system to operate.

MYTH FORTY-TWO

You cannot put kitchenettes into rooms otherwise you will be turning the rooms into flats

There is an element of truth in the above statement. There are no clear rules on this and each case comes down to how various council departments treat kitchenettes in rooms. The council departments who are usually involved are: the Housing Standards, Planning, and Council Tax departments. The least of a landlord's worries is the Housing Standards Department. They often encourage the provision of extra facilities for tenants, their sole concern is safety, and from experience, they want:

The kitchenettes positioned away from the door as they consider any form of cooking to be a fire hazard, which could prevent the tenants escaping from the room.

The smoke detector in the room being replaced by a heat detector, as cooking in the room will cause false alarms. Also, a stand-alone mains-operated battery back-up smoke detector, with an accessible hush button, should fitted in the room to give early warning of fire.

A fire blanket is supplied and fitted near the cooking facilities. Very few councils now demand fire extinguishers as they could be considered to place a tenant in danger. The same logic does not seem to apply to fire blankets.

The kitchenette is to have an extractor fitted, although it is not clear whether the extractor should be vented to the outside. However, I've never seen a Housing Standards officer check this, so presumably a cooker hood that recirculates the air through a filter is sufficient.

The planning department in my area will generally not take much notice of kitchenettes, provided there is also a communal kitchen and there are no fitted cooking appliances in the room, (i.e. they are all plug-in). The planners also prefer to see the kitchenette, cooker, microwave etc. in the main room, as opposed to in a separate room, as this would make the room more like a flat.

The Council Tax department could take the supply of a kitchenette as evidence of a flat and charge the room to Council Tax instead of, or as well as, charging Council Tax on the whole house as an HMO. Generally, the department takes a pragmatic view and treats a house that is split into separate bed-sitting rooms, even with en suites and kitchenettes, as one dwelling; they charge the landlord Council Tax on the whole house.

However, they have enormous discretion to do what they want, and by fitting a kitchenette you could give the council the justification to charge Council Tax on each room (though they do not need justification as they have so much discretionary power).

MYTH FORTY-THREE

You cannot charge more for a room than a flat

I apologise in advance for disappointing those who think common sense applies in this business. Most of what I call studio units (others call micro-flats or hotel-style rooms) – that is, a large room with an en suite and kitchenette – yield greater rent than flats in the locality. Why? My guess is because flats are generally unfurnished and don't include bills, while studios do. With the studio, usually the Council Tax, electric, central heating, water rates and Wi-Fi is included in the rent. I suspect the average cost of utilities, insurance and Wi-Fi for a flat would be about £60 per week.

The weekly breakdown for extra costs for a flat is as follows:

Council Tax	£20
Heating	£17
Water	£6
Electric	£12
Wi-Fi	£5
TOTAL	**£60**

The above breakdown above is only an estimate and circumstances vary widely.

From talking to tenants, the reason they give for staying in an HMO is, we are more like a hotel – easy to move into, easy to leave, and tenants do not have to worry about the cost of utilities, insurance, and Wi-Fi. Also, I do not think that tenants realise how much they would have to pay for utilities. Note, I do not wish to give them the idea that they would be better off having a flat by asking "why are you staying me if you could rent a flat for less?"

MYTH FORTY-FOUR
You cannot get a property for nothing

I have acquired properties for nothing myself and I will hopefully continue to do so. While possible, it is certainly not an every-day event to get a property for no or very little cost. Over the years, I have acquired over fifty properties for nothing and without trying. Admittedly, I did often invest money in the property to speed the renovation works up so I could let it faster, but I could have chosen not to and started by renting a few of the best rooms, using the income to improve the property so as to be able to gradually improve the property until I could let the whole property.

I have acquired many more properties for less than a few thousand pounds. I estimate that if I did work at it, I would be able to pick up a property for nothing every few months. I can show those who have the right attitude and the motivation how to do the same.

There is no special magic to obtaining properties at no cost. It is simply knowing the techniques and then taking advantage of opportunities as they arise. I agree that to acquire properties for nothing is less likely in prosperous areas but still not impossible. The techniques for obtaining properties for nothing are to use such strategies as: delayed completion, lease options, rent to rent, leases, vendor finance, and adverse possession.

Critics of these strategies say that you still need money for legal costs, stamp duty, deposits, and renovation and I agree. For most deals, you need at least £1 to prove consideration though in practice no one bothers to collect the £1. It is simply a nominal figure. However, adverse possession can be done for nothing if you can find a few sheets of paper and a marker pen. Using the contracts I have developed for most strategies, at least to start with, you can avoid legal costs.

MYTH FORTY-FIVE
You have to take a deposit when renting a property

There is no law that forces you take a deposit or prevents you from taking one. I was one of the few who stopped taking deposits before the introduction of the Tenancy Deposit Scheme because:

On principle I felt the tenancy deposit scheme was wrong, unnecessary, and anti-landlord.

The legislation was very badly drafted, and I could foresee many of the problems that have arisen since. I have been surprised that there hasn't been a PPI-like storm of ambulance-chasing lawyers, litigating their way to fortune at the expense of landlords, as for even a technical breach of the legislation a landlord can be charged four times the deposit and three times for any subsequent breach. In one recent case that went to court, a landlord had to pay his tenant nine times the deposit taken.

The proposed introduction of the tenancy deposit scheme rules made me review what I did. As often happens, what looked like a problem turned out to be a profitable marketing opportunity for me, as I advertise no deposits required and I decided to charge administration fees instead of taking deposits, which a landlord can keep. Most private landlords do not charge an administration fee: although smaller than a deposit, the fee is not refunded. I am overall better off financially in keeping the administration fee than going to the trouble of managing deposits.

I see no advantage in charging a deposit as I do not think it has much influence on most tenants' behaviour; they will either look after the property or not. I think the habit of taking deposits is so heavily ingrained into the psyche of landlords that they have never stopped to think if it is really of any benefit. Landlords assume it will stop tenants damaging a property. However, if you wish to be able to keep a deposit due to damage caused, there needs to be a thorough inventory carried out to satisfy the tenancy deposit scheme adjudicator in the event of any dispute. Inventory clerks are not cheap and if you carry out the checks yourself it takes time, so on balance it will probably cost you more than it gains.

The government are banning letting fees from April 2019. I will then have to think again and hopefully turn this into another opportunity.

MYTH FORTY-SIX

You are not allowed to let a house as rooms without permission

Permission from whom? The assumption that you cannot do anything without someone's permission is incorrect. Providing your actions do not break the law, you are allowed to do with your own property whatever you wish. What needs to be established is how you intend to let the rooms. If you are only going to use the rooms as short-term, non-permanent accommodation, called Serviced Accommodation, then Planning, Building Control, Licensing and Housing Standards should not apply, though the property must be safe. If using the property as an HMO then you must ensure the following:

a) Planning permission: unless it falls within what is called "Permitted Development," you may have problems with the planners. If they object, they can take enforcement action to stop you doing what you are doing. Providing you comply with the enforcement order, no further sanctions will result. NB: unless an Article 4 applies to your area, you are allowed under Permitted Development Rights to turn a house or flat into a small HMO for up to 6 persons.

b) Building Control: a change of use usually involves compliance with building control. With a small HMO, unless there are any alterations that involve building control, they rarely need to be involved or cause a problem.

c) Housing Standards: turning a house into an HMO will require compliance with Housing Standards. I have come up with 51 requirements that Housing Standards could require, and I am confident that there are more that I have missed or some council official will dream up.

d) Licensing: There may be a requirement to license the HMO.

e) Lenders: if there is a loan on the property, then you may require the permission of the lender to change the use of the property.

Apart from (e) above, providing you comply with the legislation, nobody can stop you doing whatever you want with your property. Should the lender object, your only choice is to re-mortgage. However, there are plenty of lenders around who do not object to you letting your property as rooms, either as an HMO or as serviced accommodation.

MYTH FORTY-SEVEN
The private sector is exploitative of tenants

The exploitation of tenants tends to be the view of left-wing minded individuals and is something I struggle to understand. I have tried to discuss it with those who hold the opinion that the private sector is exploitative, but most tend to do what I call "dump and run." They make comments, but then refuse to discuss them. It is almost as though they are frightened to discuss their opinions. Their objection seems to be that landlords make money out of housing tenants, as though this is a crime or immoral; it appears to be based on nothing more than the belief that profit and certain things do not mix. There are a huge range of other businesses – including suppliers of other basic necessities such as health services, food and clothing – who make money from basic needs, so I struggle to understand the rationale that being a landlord should be wrong and what their issue is.

What none of the objectors seem to grasp is that the private sector provides housing at a fraction of the cost of the social sector and still has to make a profit. For example, I have housed unemployed tenants for £60 per week who were previously housed by the social sector, and I have found what the social sector charges for housing them in hostels. The sector charges up to £600 a week, being 10 times what I receive. The tenants are not that complimentary about the hostel. Then again, I have had tenants leaving me to go back to the hostel because they did not like me telling them to behave; they said they did not have such restrictions in the hostel.

We in the private sector are strictly policed by Housing Standards, yet the very same Housing Standards officers ignore their own housing in the social sector and few of the regulations apply to them. The equivalent of an HMO landlord in the social sector can evict at will, without a court order, and demand that the tenant has to leave the premises immediately. I have been in a hostel discussing rehousing one of the occupants and experienced on-the-spot evictions first-hand.

It seems to me that private sector landlords are treated with an irrational prejudice that works in favour of the social sector. If you wish to operate HMOs with housing benefit tenants, then it appears you are better off registering as a social landlord.

MYTH FORTY-EIGHT

Professionals, including letting agents, can do a better job at letting an HMO than the owner

I would love to carry out my own survey centred on this myth as all the evidence I have come across thus far (which is mostly anecdotal) shows that letting agents do a bad job. I am not sure whether the criticism is reasonable as I have let HMOs for others and found some owners to be demanding, mean and irrational. Very few of what I call the unreasonable landlords have ever let properties themselves, so they fail to understand the limitations and difficulties of operating an HMO. I have acquired a few HMOs from landlords who have decided a guaranteed rent from me is better than dealing with agents. From observation of the previous very low occupancy rates and management of the property, I cannot fault the landlord and they clearly made the right decision to sack the agent. I suspect my guaranteed rent gives them more revenue than using an agent. Therefore, I must be better at letting the property than the agent, as I still have to make a profit on top of paying the landlord. I believe the opinion that agents can do a better job has been influenced by many training course providers. In order to encourage people to join their courses, they tell investors to "work on their business, not in their business." They also claim that being an HMO landlord is easy, that you can have other people manage the property. I believe they say this as a lot of people are put off being an HMO landlord by the thought of having to manage tenants – hence the emphasis on a hands-off approach to get people to join their courses. I must be the exception as I quite enjoy dealing with tenants and encourage my students to manage their HMOs. No one will ever do a better job than you will.

The conclusion I have drawn from observation is that those who manage their own HMOs seem to have greater success at it than those who use agents. The obvious counter-argument I am sure an agent would make is that a landlord is very unlikely to complain about their own inadequacies, as it goes against human nature.

MYTH FORTY-NINE

You can become financially independent through property in only 12 months

I know of people who become financially independent within months of renting a large house and sub-letting the rooms, thereby living rent- and utility-free and they still have money left over, which is always used to travel. When I have questioned them, it appears that they live on about £200 per week providing the house is fully let and every occupant pays. Even if someone is being freed from the need to pay rent and bills, living off £200 per week is not my idea of financial independence.

However, £200 is about three times the amount the unemployed live on. I suspect for the people I have met living like this, it is a lifestyle change and just a short-term escape from working in a high-pressure job. If their job was paying £50k a year, by the time they have paid tax, for travel to work, rent and utilities they are not that much worse off than working and usually have a small inheritance or savings to make up the difference. One might ask why have they not acquired a few more houses and multi-let them, which would then provide a good income. However, I suspect a steady income from the property would take longer than 12 months to establish. The other problem with the concept of financial independence is knowing, how much is enough? I suspect when people reach their original target, they look for more. If I were to set a more realistic target of, say, a gross income of £10,000 per month, I think you would have to be very efficient and lucky to yield the same figure within 12 months. A single deal often takes at least 12 months from start to finish to be income producing. I would feel more comfortable in saying financial independence could be reached within 24 months, but a very good start would have been made within 12 months. The person would also have to take on what the average investor would consider some awesome deals to make financial independence possible so early.

MYTH FIFTY

Owning property means you are rich

In the long term, if you own property, it does mean you are rich – often very rich. Property has historically doubled in value every 10 to 20 years, so if you have enough property and live long enough, you will inevitably become wealthy. In the meantime, you may have to be patient and make do. Sometimes a property can be a money pit and cost more than it makes if you are sucked into a bad deal, are unlucky, or the property is badly managed.

The risks involved are why I always tell people to look upon capital appreciation as speculation and concentrate on income. In my area (in the West Midlands) property has not increased to where it had stood pre-2008, even 10 years later, so relying on capital appreciation was not a good idea. However, if you had purchased in the South-East, even though prices have dropped in the last year, you would have still done very well, so it is fair to say that capital appreciation can be location dependent.

BONUS MYTH

You cannot do that!

I hope by the time you have read this book, you have come to the conclusion that you can do a lot more than you could possibly think with property and have realised you can achieve your goal of financial independence. The major limitation to doing anything is yourself. Once you have got out of your own way, the world is your oyster. The HMO Daddy organisation would be delighted to assist you in your journey, so if you are prepared to work hard, commit, persist, and have the stomach for the issues that arise in property, head over to **https://www.hmodaddy.com/training-events** to find out how we can help you further.

BEST OF LUCK

www.ingramcontent.com/pod-product-compliance
Lightning Source LLC
Chambersburg PA
CBHW061159180526
45170CB00002B/867